MAKE MONEY NOW!™

MONEY-MAKING OPPORTUNITIES FOR TEENS WHO LIKE PETS AND ANIMALS

PAULA JOHANSON

ROSEN PUBLISHING®

New York

For young entrepreneurs and their animal partners!

Published in 2014 by The Rosen Publishing Group, Inc.
29 East 21st Street, New York, NY 10010

Library of Congress Cataloging-in-Publication Data

Johanson, Paula.
Money-making opportunities for teens who like pets and animals/Paula Johanson.—1st ed.—New York: Rosen, c2014
    p. cm.—(Make money now!)
Includes bibliographical references and index.
ISBN 978-1-4488-9384-3
1. Animal culture—Vocational guidance—Juvenile literature. 2. Animal specialists—Vocational guidance—Juvenile literature. 3. Animal welfare—Vocational guidance—Juvenile literature. I. Title.
SF80 .J64 2014
636'.0023

Manufactured in the United States of America

CPSIA Compliance Information: Batch #S13YA: For further information, contact Rosen Publishing, New York, New York, at 1-800-237-9932.

CONTENTS

INTRODUCTION

How often do teenagers complain that there's nothing to do or that they don't have any money to have fun with? That's not the case for Bram and his sister Crystal. They've been able to turn their interest in animals into part-time work.

When Crystal sold her guinea pigs' offspring, Bram noticed that the customers didn't have cages as nice as the one he had made for his sister's pets. This moment was an opportunity! He knew what these animals needed for shelter and bedding. Bram made cages available to sell with each young pet the next time Crystal had a litter of guinea pigs ready for new homes.

It was good marketing. Customers who saw Crystal's pets in their home cage wanted to have one like it for their own animals. When a customer asked to buy a matching birdhouse, Bram realized he could build and sell birdhouses, too. He found a book of patterns for them and for birdfeeders and scarecrows.

One family hired Crystal to entertain at their toddler's birthday party. She painted animal faces on the children, sang *Old MacDonald* with them, and brought two guinea pigs that were the stars of the show. To Crystal, this event was more fun than babysitting. Crystal put up posters at the library and recreation centers to advertise her new Guinea Pig Party service. Every week that summer, she was hired to do a party for different families.

Bram and Crystal aren't the only young people looking for ways to earn money. These are just a few of the money-making opportunities for young people interested in pets and animals. Most opportunities for making money fall into two separate types. Finding a job to work for someone else will suit some teens. Other young people would rather offer a service to customers or make things to sell.

There are many suggestions for working with animals. There are options for people living far from cities, where there are farm animals and wilderness. There are also options for

Pets like these guinea pigs are more than cute animals to cuddle. There are so many money-making ways that young people can learn to care for them and make the things they need.

people in small towns and suburban settings, as well as suggestions for individuals in the downtown core of a city. It's a good idea to consider all alternatives. Many suggestions that have an urban or rural setting will apply to young people living in other areas as well. After all, country people bring their products to farmers' markets in the city. In addition, young people growing up in a big city might spend a summer on a relative's farm.

All of the places people live offer unique settings where opportunities and resources combine. Sometimes animals are the resources, and sometimes they are the opportunities for people to be caring and busy. There are plenty of choices for earning money available to young people who are willing to do the work that's needed for pets and animals where they live.

CHAPTER
1
RURAL OPPORTUNITIES

Earning money by working with animals is easier in many ways for young people living in rural and wilderness areas than it is in cities. There is loads of work to be done, especially for teenagers who can get up early in the morning and face hot days or cold nights with a positive attitude. A terrific thing about living where there are wide-open spaces is having room to work in ways that take up a lot of space, such as raising food animals or following wild animal trails. Being outdoors gives people a chance to feel like a working part of the interconnected web of all living things.

WILDERNESS WORK

For young people who like being in wilderness areas far from cities, there are good work opportunities. Hunting guides often start as young assistants or camp cooks and become guides in their teens. Licensed guides get properly trained in hunting law and the use of firearms. Some choose to be certified as guides with canoeing or kayaking skills. Many guides and hunters prefer to use cameras instead of firearms.

Working a trapline isn't just historical work. In 2012, there were still more than 150,000 trappers in the United States. According to the Montana Trappers Association, "The majority of pelts used in the world fur trade now come from farms." In Canada and the United States, fur farms are usually family-run businesses raising mink and fox. Fur farming is

Riding horses is not just a hobby—it's a skill that's useful for leading groups of visitors on trail rides. Well-trained horses can carry even first-time riders on backcountry tours.

carefully regulated for animal welfare.

A guest ranch or "dude ranch" offers vacations in isolated places. Guests ride horses and are sometimes offered the option of helping to herd cattle or horses. Workers on the ranch assist in taking care of the horses and herd animals. Trail riding guides take guests into the backcountry or show them how to do the ranch work.

In the park systems, there are good jobs for young people. A few will be hired as park ranger's assistants. Most will find summer jobs as park maintenance workers or campsite assistants cleaning picnic areas and toilets.

Any workers in wilderness areas must be considerate of the wild animals that share the same area. Following basic food safety in a tree planters' camp can help prevent attracting scavengers and may end up saving bears and coyotes from needing to be relocated or killed by animal control officers. Forest firefighters must be aware of how fires and burned ground affect the movements of wild animals.

RESCUING ANIMALS WITH SCIENCE

The science fair project of a South African teen was a great discovery. Louis Kock tested his project until he was sure his degreaser product was safe and effective for cleaning wildlife caught in oil spills. A wildlife rehabilitation center used his degreaser to wash three hundred oiled gannets and bought large quantities the next year during an oil spill. "A seventeen-year-old kid invented a product that helped save the lives of 19,000 penguins," marveled biologist Dyan deNapoli in her book about the rescue of penguins along the coast of South Africa after a devastating oil spill in 2000. "How cool is that?"

CHARISMATIC MEGAFAUNA

For many people, large animals have more appeal than small ones and insects. There's a reason why the World Wildlife Federation has a panda on its logo—pandas have faces and look cute. It's hard to imagine hugging a stickleback fish, even if it is an endangered species. Trophy hunters will stalk bighorn sheep for hours to photograph a magnificent specimen, walking right past alpine lakes where red-legged frogs are being crowded out by an invasive species of bullfrogs.

Clients hire guides to help them see interesting large mammals, not mosquitoes and slugs. Occasionally, the only charismatic megafauna around is the guide. Your charisma is part of what the client has hired. Be willing and able to show your enthusiasm for the animals in that local environment. Have a short anecdote to tell if the client asks whether you've heard any local stories. The cheerful attitude of a guide will contribute to a good experience.

There are many animal-related elements to a wilderness experience even when a large animal cannot be seen. Elk and moose leave their footprints and the broken branches from their grazing. Bears or smaller scavengers like raccoons are a constant concern in some areas. As the garbage from lunch is carefully handled for proper disposal, or a food bag is hung from a high tree branch every night, the guide has opportunities to show clients how awareness of animals is affecting the people on this wilderness experience.

FARM WORK

In rural areas, many young people work with their parents on the home farm or find work with relatives for the summer. Some teens work to earn an allowance, whereas others work to earn a wage. Farming families are often very supportive of a young person's interest in working with animals, either joining the family business or setting up a small independent project. Assistance and advice can come from relatives and neighbors or employers as well as a young person's parents. Teenagers whose family farms produce grain or vegetables can find work with animals on the nearby farms and ranches of neighbors.

On a ranch or cattle farm, young workers help with beef cattle, herding the cows and calves into fenced pastures. At a dairy farm, teenagers can help with milking the cows and caring for the calves. Bulls are so big and temperamental that many farmers rely on artificial insemination to breed their cows. Young workers on a sheep farm care for the flock, herding sheep into fenced pastures, shearing wool, and hand-raising a few of the lambs. Chicken farm laborers can work raising chickens for meat or raising them to lay eggs.

Much of the work of raising food animals is simple and involves repetitive chores. This kind of work is well-suited to a strong teenager working part-time, after school, or on weekends.

There's always plenty of work to be found on a farm, caring for sheep and other animals. Many farm chores are suitable for young people, who are still growing and learning.

Large animals have special needs. They may be too big or strong for a young person to handle alone at first, but experience and a good attitude will help as time goes on.

DIRTY WORK

Any young worker on a farm or ranch is likely to be asked to handle animal manure. Chicken farm workers clear dirty straw off the floor of a chicken house. Workers in a dairy use a water hose to clean the milking room floor. After driving pigs to an auction, a worker cleans the back of the truck.

Handling animal manure is just part of the job. Everyone in farm work does it. The person in charge did this work—and probably still does. And if on some farms, teenagers do all the work handling manure, it's because they are strong and might not be experienced at operating machinery. Meanwhile, the experienced adults are operating heavy equipment carefully.

A sensible worker learns to do dirty work with good-will instead of complaining the whole time. Wear coveralls or old clothes, gloves, and perhaps a mask to keep from breathing too much dust, and get to it! Afterward, wash yourself clean and be proud of a job well done. The boss will appreciate a good attitude. It will be very obvious just how hard you are working.

This work is actually very important for keeping the animals healthy and keeping barns usable. Many farms practice sustainable resource management by using manure for compost. Composted manure is good for the soil in gardens and fields.

FARM VETERINARIAN'S ASSISTANT

A farm veterinarian specializes in the care of large farm animals and often cares for a few dogs and cats as well. Some large animal vets work with wild animal rescue or rehabilitation. Vet assistants work as receptionists and clean the clinic and cages or stables where animals are kept overnight. Vets need assistants to help control a large animal during treatment.

Assisting a farm vet requires strength and confidence. Experience handling cattle, horses, pigs, and sheep is essential. Exotic

Assisting a farm veterinarian is a hands-on job, out in the field or at a clinic. Assistants learn by doing, with vets showing how to handle animals, equipment, and feed.

animals such as ostriches or alpacas and llamas require special handling. An assistant can expect a few bruises and scratches, but a careless worker could be badly hurt by animals that panic.

PROJECTS FOR THE 4-H CLUB

Teenagers who look after a steer, a sheep, or a pig for a 4-H Club program learn every step of the process of raising animals for harvest. First, each teen buys a young animal at auction. They nurture their own animals, keeping records of all expenses, including feed and veterinary care. Then the grown animals are sold at auction or brought to a slaugh-terhouse so that the cut and wrapped meat can be sold to a customer. These programs are terrific training for becoming a rancher.

The 4-H Club helps young people learn how to raise and market animals humanely. Often auction houses consider animals raised for 4-H projects to be the finest animals that they sell.

WORKING IN
WATER ENVIRONMENTS

There are many jobs working with fish and other marine life. Some young people are hired for a week or a summer to work on fishing boats, such as trollers with fishing lines or trawlers with nets or for crab-fishing. It's possible to get a fishing license and a small boat and then bring in a few fish at a time to a cannery or a local restaurant. Look into the rules for small-scale commercial fishing in your area. There are also land-based jobs in container fish farming or as an assistant in a fish hatchery.

At marinas, there are opportunities to be hired as a marina assistant. The duties range from cleaning fish and selling fuel for boat engines to selling fishing licenses or fishing rods and tackle and renting or maintaining boats. Whale-watching tours need the boats and waterproof suits to be cleaned after every trip.

Young people can also be hired as fishing guides. Be aware that there's a common option of "catch-and-release" in many areas. Learn what fish are living in local streams and lakes. Is that trout a brook, cutthroat, rainbow, or a bull trout? Clients will want to know.

Any boat operator has safety concerns, for both people and animals. Government rules for boating safety include having a lifejacket or personal flotation device for each person aboard, as well as rope and a bailer. The fishing guide is responsible for steering the canoe or operating the boat's motor. If you choose to earn money as a fishing guide, take care with boat motors so that you don't injure animals in a collision or by spilling fuel into the water.

VOLUNTEER OPPORTUNITIES

Workers in the international program World Wide Opportunities on Organic Farms are called WWOOFers. The program offers good experience in working with farm animals in exchange for room and board and can lead to ongoing jobs. Young people choose where they want to work and for how many months. They live with their host family and work a prearranged number of part-time hours. WWOOFers under the age of eighteen must be accompanied by a guardian.

Other volunteer opportunities include building and maintaining wilderness trails and mountain shelters in bear country with the Sierra Club and other groups. This type of volunteer work can give young people the experience of working around wild animals, which might improve their chance of employment in government park maintenance programs.

In small towns, there are many small business development opportunities for teens who like pets and animals. Keeping a flock of free-range chickens in the yard makes sense when there are neighbors to buy eggs. Instead of raising a couple of turkeys for family Thanksgiving and Christmas dinners, it's a good idea to raise a dozen or more for customers who appreciate birds raised using cruelty-free methods.

Trimming pet claws can keep a teenager working every weekend for a series of pet owners. Look around at what people need and at the options you have. Some of the small town

It's not hard to build chicken houses, keep them clean, or sell the chickens' eggs. Chickens eat garden weeds, kitchen waste, and grain. It's good to have eggs, meat, and also composted manure for gardens.

opportunities discussed here will work for teens living in cities or rural areas as well.

SPACE FOR DOGS

To the new owner of a puppy that cost hundreds of dollars, breeding dogs can seem like a good way to earn money. A successful breeder of Havanese dogs, Bev Dorma was thrilled when her dog won Best in Breed at the 136th Westminster Kennel Club Dog Show in New York City. Dorma can sell a healthy puppy for about $1,800. But she told *Boulevard* magazine, "It's not something you make money at." That price tag is high because each puppy sold has passed expensive health and genetic testing. Dorma considers her show dog breeding to be a hobby that pays for itself, not a career that supports all the costs of her household. She is proud that six generations of her dogs are healthy and long-lived. Animal breeders have to be careful that the people who buy their young animals will give them good homes. Selling puppies can help a teenager save money for college, but it rarely earns enough to support a family home.

CHAMBER OF COMMERCE

A good place to find help in making your own animal-related employment is through Junior Achievers, or Junior Chamber of Commerce, and other programs organized by your local chamber of commerce. These programs teach young entrepreneurs to develop their own products, such as cat toys, or services, such as dog grooming. Participants are shown how to start a small business, learn marketing techniques, keep records, and fill out legal forms. Meeting with other small businesspeople is fun and interesting, and it can help you network for future jobs.

Young dog owners can earn money training dogs for obedience trials, where dogs follow commands over a course at a show. Some trainers work to train the owners as much as the dogs, while other trainers are hired by owners to exercise the dogs and to handle them at shows.

Another income source for young dog owners is operating a kennel or a dog hotel, working from their family homes and yards. Kennels with fenced yards offer space for exercise and supervised play with the young kennel operator. Some kennels even offer day spa services for dogs.

FENCING

Look around small town communities for fences appropriate to the animals being kept, whether they are fowl, sheep, horses, cattle, bison, or pigs. These fences need maintenance. People building new homes and yards need new fences. Here are opportunities for teenagers to meet neighbors who need work done.

A handy teen with gloves and a few tools can assist on large projects and complete small projects or maintenance alone. Portable fences or large cages can be made for using a flock of chickens to weed part of a garden or field. There are designs available in books and on the Internet. Remember that fencing deer, rabbits, or coyotes *out* of a garden is another kind of skill.

LIVESTOCK WORK AS ANIMAL HANDLERS

Livestock auction houses sell a variety of farm animals. Fowl are usually sold weekly on Saturdays with small and medium-sized animals such as pigs, goats, and sheep. Exotic animals such as ostriches and llamas used to be a rare sight

DESIGNER

When she was a teenager on her aunt and uncle's farm in Arizona, Temple Grandin believed that she understood the cattle they were raising. As a high-functioning autistic teen, Grandin found it hard to handle crowds of people, but she was very good at the work of feeding and caring for cattle. Her work in handling farm animals led her to her university studies and eventually to earning a doctorate in animal science. Now she designs efficient and humane slaughterhouses that control the movement of animals, keeping them calm and preventing injuries, and works with the livestock industry to improve their methods for livestock handling.

but are becoming more common. Auction houses often sell cattle or horses on a separate day of the week. The main work for teenagers at livestock auctions is as animal handlers. These handlers bring out each cage of chickens or lead each llama forward as the auction manager calls the lot number.

For trucking firms, animal handlers load farm animals into trucks. The animals are then shipped to auction houses and slaughterhouses. Drivers should be licensed to drive large trucks with air brakes. There are laws for driving and age restrictions in many states—to obtain a commercial driver's license in most states, a person needs to be at least eighteen years old.

Family members who raise animals and birds on a family farm for food for the family may butcher the animals themselves. But animals and birds raised for sale must be butchered in a slaughterhouse and inspected before being approved for sale. In

At auction houses, animal handlers have to be quick and strong. A calm, confident handler helps animals to be calm, too. That's especially important when handling a lot of large animals!

slaughterhouses, young people work as animal handlers and janitors.

Working in a privately owned small slaughterhouse is probably a more positive experience than working in a large slaughterhouse. Unlike most other careers in agriculture, the dangers of working in a large slaughterhouse have not decreased with modern technology but rather increased. Enforcement of animal cruelty laws means that conditions for animals at slaughterhouses have improved in some ways since the year 2000. "Conditions for slaughterhouse workers, however, have deteriorated," according to food safety writer Erik Markus. Smaller, privately owned slaughterhouses are usually cleaner workplaces, much safer for the employees, and sometimes the only workplace for miles around.

WORKING WITH HORSES

There is plenty of work for young people in stables, from teaching riding lessons to assisting in riding programs for children who have disabilities. Teens can run a horse boarding operation to keep a stable and paddocks busy, where people rent stalls to keep their horses. No one will board a horse in someone else's stable without being confident that there are stable lads on site to take care of the horses if the owners have an emergency and cannot be present every day. Stable lads clean the stalls and give horses feed and water. They could also assist equine sports therapists in caring for horses that are recovering from injuries.

At stables where racehorses are raised, trainers hire work jockeys or exercise jockeys. These young people, who are age sixteen and older, ride racehorses and steeplechasers in training. A few go on to become pro-fessional jockeys in races.

Old-fashioned skills are still being used in some places. There are still farriers, shoeing horses and tending their hooves. Young assistants can learn this skill set. Even plow horses are still being trained today. A teenager who learns farrier skills can perform them for demonstrations at heritage festivals and historic replica villages or museums, such as the Farmer's Museum in Cooper-stown, New York. Many horseshoeing/farrier schools require students to be at least seventeen years old to attend their programs.

There's lots of work around a stable. Clean stalls, fresh water, and a tidy paddock keep horses healthy. Cleaning up horse manure is no problem for most people who love horses.

WALKING TRAILS

If you've walked all over town, you've probably seen every example of local habitat for animals. Approach the town manager and facilities manager about a job making an animal theme trail around town, similar to the walking tours in Bozeman, Montana, and Chicago, Illinois. Based on your knowledge of local animals, map a route past local businesses to a local nature center and other places where walkers can see animal habitats, such as streams, thickets, or parks with trees. There should be interpretive signs. Viewpoints of mountains or river valleys are another good element for a trail, like the ones in Denver, Colorado, and Banff in Alberta, Canada. Get permission to stencil an animal logo on sidewalks or roads along the route, as the trails are marked in San Francisco, California, and Jacksonville, Florida. (To get some helpful ideas for stenciled trails, check out a project that high school students completed with the Brookton Walk Trail in Western Australia [http://www.canwa.com.au/articles/news/brookton-trail-of-art-launch].)

VOLUNTEER OPPORTUNITIES: ANIMAL RESCUE AND REHABILITATION

Animal lovers care for more than their own pets. Injured wild animals are saved by the hard work of many volunteers led by a few biologists and their trained assistants. Animal rescue or rehabilitation societies usually hire their few paid workers from among their volunteers. According to biologist Dyan deNapoli, "Most zoos and aquariums hire new staff from their volunteer and intern pools." Experience as a volunteer in animal activism and parks protection can help teenagers improve their chances to be hired by the Sierra Club and rehabilitation societies or as park maintenance workers in government parks programs.

CHAPTER 3

SUBURBAN OPPORTUNITIES

In the suburbs, young people live within walking distance of many possible customers and employers, or they are only a short ride away by bike or bus. Although there may not be farm animals nearby, there are plenty of money-making opportunities for working with pets and other animals. Some of these opportunities will be available in small towns and big cities as well.

Try expanding a babysitting business by organizing pet-themed or animal-themed camps for children during spring or summer break. A teenager starting his or her first business can do market research in person among thousands of potential customers in a suburb. Remember that an ethical business does not pester people who might be clients—ads belong in local or online newspapers and on bulletin boards, not covering every wall and telephone pole in a neighborhood! Remember, too, your personal safety—a library or a local business fair are both good public places for meeting a future employer or customer.

DOG HANDLING

What work with pets and animals can young people do? Almost the first thing that comes to mind is dog walking. Buy a good leash, make friends with a few neighbors, and check out the nearest park . . . it sounds easy. Earning money just for walking around with a dog is simple.

But there's a lot more that a good dog handler can do to improve this work. With a little training and good brushes and

Grooming pets properly for a show takes time and practice. Even scruffy pets benefit from good care for their coats, paws, and teeth by considerate groomers who do the job well.

clippers, it's easy to learn dog grooming. It takes effort to get good at bathing dogs, but some owners will make regular appointments, especially for large dogs. Anyone who can successfully bathe cats is likely to have a few regular customers who are very grateful.

For a fee of about $25 or $30, a young person can ask the local police department or the FBI to do a criminal record check and confirm that he or she is bondable. A young person, with written references from satisfied customers in hand, can be endorsed by a community association or the local neighborhood watch program. This kind of acknowledgment will encourage neighbors to allow a reliable teenager to enter their homes as a house sitter while the neighbors are away at work or on vacation. As well as walking their dogs, cleaning a cat's litter box, or feeding their budgies or fish, a reliable house sitter will bring in the neighbor's mail and confirm that the home is secure.

BIRD-WATCHING TOURS AND NATURE GUIDES

Any good bird-watcher soon learns the best places near home to see birds and which species are likely to be found. Other animals and plants are interesting to see on hikes through local parks.

31

Teen birders can put this knowledge to good use. Bird-watchers can be found in the downtown core of big cities, in suburbs, in small towns, and even visiting wilderness areas, and they are all potential customers because they might be looking for local knowledge about where the good places are to look for birds.

A young bird-watcher will be able to learn all the facts needed to make a local bird-watching pamphlet or booklet, with information on local species and a map of good places to see birds. Depending on the bird-watcher's skills, this booklet could be on paper or an electronic version to read on computers and smartphones, perhaps as a PDF file or a Web site. Plan a short tour that can take under an hour and a longer tour that can take all afternoon.

Local hotels and bed-and-breakfast places are often looking for information to give to their guests about nearby activities. Some hotel managers will

Bird-watchers often have expensive binoculars, cameras, and other equipment. Smart guides for bird-watching will carry a packet of lens-wiping tissues as well as pocket editions of books that identify birds.

hire a guide to lead hotel guests on tours. Recreation centers and public libraries hire people to lead activities. Posters can be displayed at shopping centers and schools. With a little planning and promotion, a young person can lead bird-watching tours and nature walks every weekend year-round or several days each week during the summer.

WILD ANIMAL RELOCATION

Teens have many opportunities for an afternoon of work when neighbors need help relocating wild animals. It's sensible for teenagers to meet neighbors and ask them for part-time work keeping their yards from being an attractive nuisance to wild animals. When called on to remove a bird's nest or evict squirrels, these teens think about the animal's needs as well as the human's. In some areas, coyotes or cougars might be a worry. In autumn, fallen fruit from trees can attract bears. A savvy teen finds enough clients to keep busy every weekend all year—and knows to call the district's animal control officers when a dangerous animal is on the scene.

Getting to know the neighbors, both human and animal, can really pay off. Many people do not want to deal with the hassle of using mousetraps, rat traps, or poison. With care, a teenager can handle these things safely, without endangering children or pet dogs and cats. A young person who buys a live trap can use it many times when removing raccoons or opossums from yards. Try to get referrals to new customers whenever possible.

ANIMAL PARTY PLANNER

A teenager with several pets can become a local service for hosting animal-themed parties. Where there are a lot of people and children, there are a lot of parties, particularly children's parties. The guests could come to the yard where the animals live or another location where the animals are brought for the event in suitable cages. The party planner can prepare a number of animal-themed activities, such as games and crafts. Songs, stories, and face painting can be interesting and fun.

This young assistant is helping a vet with record keeping at a small clinic. There are many tasks that clinic receptionists perform, including caring for animals, keeping the office and boarding facilities clean, and working with the public.

ASSISTANT TO SMALL ANIMAL VETERINARIANS

In towns and cities, veterinarians usually specialize in small animals rather than large farm animals. Young assistants can work as receptionists, help keep the clinic clean, or look after animals that have been boarded overnight. Familiarity with exotic animals is an asset, as an assistant might be called on to hold an iguana or maintain a tarantula habitat.

ANIMAL-RELATED CRAFTS

Sometimes people who are handy or artistic will think of ways to make money using their knowledge about animals. These crafts can be sold at farmers' markets or directly to clients. Consider what kinds of items your customers might need or what their animals might need, such as:

- Dog beds, cat scratching posts, bird perches, bird feeders
- Cloth items such as ferret slings, dog jackets, car safety belts for dogs
- Saddle blankets and rugs for horses
- Collars, leashes, harnesses, halters, bridles, horse tack, saddles
- Chew toys for dogs, feathered teasers for cats, mirrors and bells for birds
- Healthy treats and bundles of chewing sticks for rodents
- Toad houses, bat houses, mason bee houses, and grazing cages
- Animal portraits

For instance, if there are several bed-and-breakfast operators in town, a young person could approach each owner about putting wild bird feeders in each of their yards. The feeders could suit the birds in that area, whether they are hummingbirds,

FOOLING WASPS

Teenagers hired to remove wasp or hornet nests know to proceed with care. The stings can be painful. The next step is to be sure that clients get their money's worth by putting up a decoy to keep another nest from being started in the same place. Unlike duck decoys, which encourage ducks to come close to the model of a duck, a decoy wasp nest discourages visiting wasps from lingering. You could buy a $10 replica nest at a garden supply store. But it's more cost-effective to stuff a brown paper bag and tie the neck so the bag is shaped like a wasp's nest. Hang it in or near the place where the real nest was just removed. Clients will appreciate this frugal and proactive effort. It's not foolproof, but it's worth a try.

phoebes, or orioles. A really smart teen could make each feeder suit each house by painting it the right colors.

VOLUNTEER OPPORTUNITIES

"I believe that it is important to link art and science when it comes to sharing knowledge about the environment," said Diane Clapp in *Canadian Wildlife* magazine. Donations of her animal-themed art are on display in nature centers, bringing her work to the attention of potential customers. For teens interested not only in animals but also in planning events, there are other choices. At Christmas, some charities will set up a booth for taking photographs of pets with Santa Claus at a local pet store or mall. A young photographer who can keep animals calm will earn a modest share of the donations collected. Moreover, a community's nature centers, dog shows at local parks, and cat shows at local halls all need volunteer organizers. These experiences can lead to work with professional animal shows or with event-planning businesses.

CHAPTER 4

URBAN OPPORTUNITIES

Young people living in a big city are not going to keep a horse or raise a flock of turkeys for Thanksgiving in the backyard. The house or apartment building may not even have a backyard. But there are other money-making opportunities available to young people who live in urban areas and who are interested in pets and animals.

PET CAREGIVER

In cities, many apartment and condo buildings do not allow residents to have dogs and cats or pets of any kind. But there are still ways to spend time with animals, without owning a pet. A pet caregiver visits other buildings to serve a variety of clients. Daily or weekly visits may be needed to meet all the pets' needs. Caregiving goes beyond walking dogs and cleaning a cat's litter box. Rodents, birds, and exotic pets need care, too.

Maintaining animal habitats can be done in commercial buildings and offices as well as private homes. Young people can offer their services to building managers and to companies with animal habitats in the lobbies of their office spaces. Terrariums need careful maintenance to keep the exotic pets living in these small habitats healthy. Aquariums need an experienced person to set up and maintain tropical fish tanks or saltwater tanks. Teens who have the knowledge and talent for working with fish tanks can advise clients to confirm their insurance needs concerning possible water damage if the tank ever leaks.

The dangerous looking moray is shy and would rather hide than attack.

Looking after a fish tank or exotic animal habitat, such as this eel's, isn't always easy. Some animals eat pelleted food neatly. Others eat live prey! It can be a challenge to keep animal habitats clean.

Pet owners will trust advice from caregivers who are members of recognized associations such as the Federation of American Aquarium Societies.

ANIMAL COURIER

Many pet owners find it hard to run their own errands. Teens who wish to set up their own business can become an animal courier and can pick up pet food and other supplies from specialty stores and deliver it right to the pet owner's door. Animal couriers can also make money by delivering the animal to a vet appointment or to a groomer or by picking up the pet from doggie day care at the end of the day. Some divorced dog owners often hire couriers to transport shared pets.

The best place to advertise animal courier services is at veterinarian's offices, animal hospitals, and pet supply stores. The courier can deliver pet prescriptions on occasion for vets, as well as food and other pet supplies for pet owners.

CARRIAGE DRIVER

In many cities, such as Atlanta, Austin, Boston, Charleston, Chicago, New Orleans, New York City, Salt Lake City, and San Francisco, horse-drawn carriages take passengers on quiet rides through a city park, along streets that don't have much traffic, or for special events. Other tours are operated by bed-and-breakfast operations in small towns. The drivers are usually teenagers who work at stables and have learned to drive a carriage in traffic. Confidence handling horses is not the only skill needed. The horses need to be groomed well, with decorative harness and tack. Tact and confidence are important qualities for a carriage driver to possess when dealing with tourists.

A horse-drawn carriage drives by a cottage on Michigan's Mackinac Island. Caring for horses is old-fashioned work that is still interesting in a modern world. Have answers ready for a client's questions, to tell about the animals and why you chose to do this kind of work.

ANIMAL STREET PERFORMER

Some performers work with dogs and other animals, doing tumbling and small tricks to entertain groups at festivals and parties. Sometimes a festival hires performers, and sometimes the performer passes a hat to collect small donations. Buskers perform at festivals and farmers' markets, where such performances will be enjoyed and expected.

Approach the event organizers to arrange permission to perform. Performers must obey child labor laws and should inquire about a street performer's license at the local city hall or chamber of commerce. The cost for a license or permit is usually less than $50 annually, although it can cost more in some places.

TRAINING ANIMAL GUIDES

There are animals trained to help people with special needs, such as helper monkeys for people who are paralyzed. Young volunteers can raise dog guides (both Seeing-Eye dogs and hearing dog guides) in their homes for the first year. With experience, some volunteers become apprentice trainers who prepare dog guides for their duties, usually hired by the Lions Foundation or the International Guide Dog Federation. Companion animals of other kinds, including ferrets and cats, are trained mostly to behave well in public by animal therapy professionals and their volunteer assistants.

ANIMAL ACTIVISM

Many jobs working for animal rights groups or animal welfare groups are minimum wage jobs. But these jobs often involve useful abilities such as office skills, fund-raising, or research assistant work. Experience working for an animal activism group such as Greenpeace or Ducks Unlimited can lead a young person to obtain excellent references and scholarships for further education or employment with other agencies. Other young activists go on from the Society for the Prevention of Cruelty to Animals (SPCA) or the Sierra Club to take an interest in a political career.

ANIMAL CARE ASSISTANT

In cities, the biggest issue of animal care is spaying and neutering of cats and dogs. Some charities offer affordable spaying or neutering. A few will do it for free when stray animals are brought to the center. These animal care clinics rely on volunteers and as few paid employees as possible. Young people can easily find work in these places, but at minimum wage, doing office work, fund-raising, or as a volunteer cleaning cages and exercising animals.

PETTING ZOO

For a teenager, a petting zoo has many opportunities for work, during a special event, a summer job, or year-round. The animals need to be fed, and their shelters need to be cleaned. Most of all, someone will have to show children how to touch or feed the animals and watch that tired animals get a place to rest where they are not bothered. These are jobs usually done by teenagers for minimum wage. Some petting zoos, however, have only one paid manager organizing a team of volunteers.

ANIMAL HANDLING ON CAMPUS

There are a surprising number of animals living on the campuses of universities and colleges. Laboratories hold a variety of animals, from white rats to amoebas and other microscopic life.

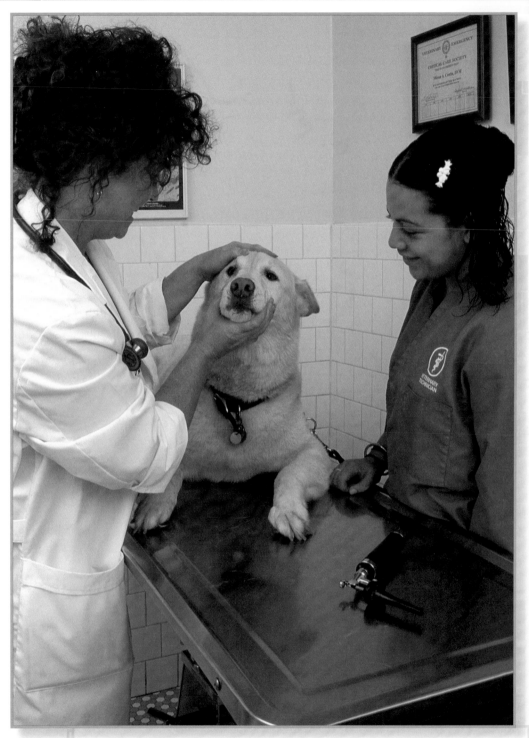

A teen volunteer watches a veterinarian check a yellow Labrador on an exam table. Volunteer work can help people decide whether they want to pursue a career caring for animals or having an animal-related business.

Some campuses have experimental farms, where chickens, pigs, cattle, and other farm animals are raised along with gardens and fields of crops. There are very strict rules about the treatment of animals for research, to avoid cruelty. Young people can often be hired for part-time or summer programs through university extension opportunities or the biology department, feeding these animals or cleaning cages and barns, and making records of the animal's condition.

On many campuses, there are summer camps and spring break camps for teens to learn about animal-related sciences. These programs are excellent opportunities to learn about animals in the context of biology or agriculture and other sciences. Teenagers are often hired as junior counselors and small group leaders for these programs. The young workers earn excellent references, which can make it much easier to obtain a scholarship for college or university. The experience will also look good on a résumé.

VOLUNTEER OPPORTUNITIES

The local branch of the SPCA always needs volunteers. At the SPCA, there's more to do than just cleaning dog kennels and cat cages. Volunteers are needed to walk the dogs, for training and to give them exercise. The cats and dogs need attention from these volunteers, who will play with them. Small pets such as chinchillas or guinea pigs particularly need to be handled by experienced volunteers so the animals become used to people. This kind of volunteer work is excellent for anyone considering a career working with animals. Volunteering for a few days each month will give solid hands-on experience to a young teenager. After volunteering, it will be so much more realistic to start your own dog kennel or spa or to have the goal of becoming a small animal vet. Serving on an SPCA committee can also help young people network with possible employers in the community.

5
BUSINESS PLANNING

When making a business plan for working with animals, start by setting goals. What will be your short-term goals for the day, week, month, or season? Think about what you need to be prepared and what you can achieve. Consider the needs of animals and owners. Think about long-term planning for next year and beyond.

GAINING SKILLS

List the skills that are needed to do your particular kind of work with animals. How will you learn these skills? Often the only way to gain a skill is through practice or by consulting experts. Some skills are taught in school or in short courses through

A computer teacher helps students with a technology course. Acquiring the right skills for starting a business includes business planning, record keeping, and management, and they are taught in many places. These skills apply to many kinds of work.

community colleges, libraries, and recreation centers. Any tuition that you must pay is a business expense for your records.

Computer skills can be a surprisingly big part of working with animals. It's convenient to own a computer but not necessary. Computer use is free in public libraries and so are computer courses that are offered there. Libraries circulate books on animal/pet-related careers and businesses, computer books, and animal and pet care.

RESOURCE MANAGEMENT

Make a list of all the resources you require and how each necessity is met. Small businesses might not need separate phone numbers from the family phone. But right from the start, there should be an e-mail address used only for your business.

A small business often uses space in a family-owned or rented property. Sometimes relatives don't charge for the use of their space and electric power. If that is the case for you, remember that you should be considerate. Keep the space tidy and store materials neatly. When the business expands to make enough profit, make sure you pay rent and keep the receipts as a business expense.

SETTING A FAIR PRICE

When setting prices for animal-related products or services, start by calculating your costs. Make lists of expenses. Consider how much time you spend doing simple actions or complicated ones. Compare your products to other products available to customers. Compare your services to what is available in other locations. It's sensible to set a competitive price, instead of twice or half the price for similar goods or services. If you need to earn more money, don't just charge your customers more. Add value to your products or services.

It's not too hard to keep track of business planning, expenses, income, and each day's work. Outline goals for the activities you want to do and the results you want to see.

COMPARING PROFITS TO INCOME GOALS

People who have different goals about money and animals feel successful with different amounts of money or different ways animals are affected. Succeeding at goals makes workers feel good, even after a tiring or boring day.

Income goals for young people are usually smaller than income goals for adults. Working adults are generally trying to earn enough money for food and shelter, as well as health care and clothing and transportation. Young people who live at home with family most likely will have many of those costs covered. A teenager might be working to save for college tuition fees or to buy a good bicycle, a computer, or first vehicle.

The profit from a young person's job or business is usually small compared to a job that earns a living to support a family home. But even a small profit might be enough to meet the young person's goals and needs, and that is a good start to a career. Furthermore, work with animals is often very emotionally satisfying.

PROMOTION

After starting a business, it's a good idea to expand your customer base. New clients could include other nearby animal owners, owners of other kinds of animals, or people living in other communities. Promotion doesn't have to involve buying a lot of expensive ads. Approach local newspapers or radio and television stations about being interviewed. Social media such as Twitter and Facebook can be useful for networking, advertising, and event announcements. Coordinate your posts and promotions with local events and other small businesses. Often several local small businesses will

SEIZE THE DAY

Working for yourself isn't like winning the lottery one day and going on vacation the rest of the year. Every day has rewarding opportunities, not only for work but also for ways to enjoy the work and keep getting the job done. It can be very satisfying to keep animals alive and well and healthy. Work with animals provides many ways to be proud, confident, and effective so that a young person learns to work hard, not only for money, but also to meet goals.

do their promotion together on a larger resource Web site run by a local magazine or business, such as the Web site for Pike Place Market in Seattle, Washington. Joining a Web site of this kind is a good way to network, reach customers, and avoid Internet predators. If you start a blog, remember to add links to animal resources from other Web sites.

OBEYING THE LAW

There are many laws to obey when working, even if you are volunteering. Child labor laws ensure that children and teenagers under eighteen years old can work only if it does not interfere with going to school and getting proper care. In some jurisdictions, youths between fourteen and sixteen years old are not allowed to do certain kinds of work, especially with large animals or machinery, or to work for long hours. Animal safety laws and animal control bylaws are meant to protect both animals and humans. There are some variations of these laws in federal, state, or local governments. Check what laws are in effect in your area so that you can meet all of your responsibilities.

Keep records and receipts for all expenses and income. A young person filling out an income tax form will usually be considered a dependent on a parent's income tax return. Even if there is not enough net income to have to pay any federal or state taxes, it's still good record keeping to fill out all the forms.

Zoning bylaws determine what kinds of business may operate in different areas. For instance, pig farms can't be started in a national park. On a residential street, a dog day care business that has a lot of noisy barking or car traffic, for example, will also have complaints from neighbors. A business must fit in well with the area where it operates, or it will be closed by the city or state.

FACING CHARGES

Breaking the law has serious consequences for people of any age. The same laws that permit a business to operate will be enforced to protect people and animals, even if a business is small. It's good business ethics to declare all of your income, do honest work, and be careful that no people or animals are harmed.

When people break the laws for operating a business, or the animal welfare laws, the punishments can be fines or even prison sentences. A person convicted of breaking laws that protect animal welfare can be barred from owning or working with animals for five or ten years. Convicted criminals can find it very difficult to be hired for work with government funding. A sensible business operator will meet all the legal requirements.

BEING PREPARED

Teens working with animals, especially in their own business, should be ready for unpredictable things like illness or accidents. Insurance agents and bank advisers can help with general liability insurance policies. Consult the local chamber of commerce for advice about whether your type of

For advice when starting a small business, look to family members and experienced businesspeople. Advisers at banks and chambers of commerce can help young entrepreneurs manage a business well.

small business needs other kinds of insurance. Young people who are self-employed in a small business at home can ask their parents if their homeowner's insurance covers the small business as well—the insurance agent will confirm it.

Teens who work with animals should also be prepared for emergencies, such as accidents or natural disasters. Take a first-aid course, not only for people but also for animals. Prepare an emergency kit—a knapsack with essential supplies for humans and pets—in case of earthquakes or evacuations. It is good business to have an associate who does similar work so you can cover for each other because animals need care every day, even when people get sick.

CHAPTER
6
CAREER BUILDING

There are many ways in which a young person's experience working with pets and other animals can help to build a career. A part-time or summer job with animals can be the first step to deciding to become a veterinarian and planning a lifelong career. It's certainly an opportunity to learn new skills when possible. There's nothing like experience cleaning up after animals or managing their behaviors to let young people know if this is the kind of work they want to do for more than a summer. Even if you plan to become a research scientist or marine biologist, expect that years after earning a university degree you will still handle lab animals or wild animals on a routine basis.

LOCAL LEARNING

There can be many opportunities to learn about animals in the local community without traveling far away to complete university degrees at great expense. Even when a small town has no university, technical institute, or community college with an agricultural or animal-related certificate program, there are other options. Distance learning programs will offer some courses. There might be a course in the university extension or community learning program in a nearby city. A lecture or a complete course can be held in a school, recreation center, or community hall, with the instructor coming to each session. The district home economist can set up a teaching session, if a few young people ask.

Experienced dog walkers can take more than a single dog around the block. It's challenging to handle several dogs at once, exercising their bodies and improving their social skills.

55

When setting up an animal-related business, talk to the local chamber of commerce about business development programs in town or nearby communities. There might be a course on taxes for small businesses that you can attend nearby. If they are asked, local community organizations will often sponsor a workshop or organize an event.

ANIMAL-RELATED SKILLS

Education opens up opportunities for anyone working with animals and sometimes in unexpected ways. Ranchers and farmers need to keep records, so a young assistant who gets good grades at school in reading and writing or math can be a real asset. Being able to keep records is an essential skill when starting any career in the sciences or working with animals.

A young person who moves on to an office job can still care about animals. Lobbyists, lawyers, accountants, and activists put office skills to good use in the service of animal welfare and agricultural or environmental concerns. Workers can

Young people can be hired to work in many ways for the benefit of animals, assisting in research and record keeping that allows scientists and lawyers to complete important projects.

consider their animal awareness to be another work-related skill, no matter where they work. What animal lover working in a sign-making shop would ever pour paint thinner down a storm drain? Instead, he or she would be more likely to ask the manager to help sponsor the Boy Scouts program to paint fish symbols on curbs above storm drains, reminding people of animal habitats downstream.

PROFESSIONAL HOUSE-SITTING

A teenager who looks after the pets and homes of neighbors can develop this skill into a career as a house sitter. Some house sitters visit a client's home, or several clients' homes, each day to look after the house and pets. This experience can lead to an adult career as a professional house sitter. These caretakers live in the home while the clients are away on vacation or traveling for business. For instance, adult house sitters can end up maintaining saltwater aquariums in a downtown condo while attending college classes or keeping a flock of sheep at a sheep station in Australia for a working vacation.

TRAINING IN ANIMAL HANDLING

Some young people have a knack for training or handling animals well. There are books on dog training at the public library. Lessons on dog obedience training are often offered through local pet stores, recreation centers, or kennel clubs. After completing courses, a young person can become qualified to teach others how to handle their own pets. Starting as an assistant, a young person can go on to learn how to teach specialized training for dog shows or obedience trials. With experience and practice, a young person could look forward to building a career as an animal handler for the film and television industries.

GRANT APPLICATIONS

One of the benefits of joining an animal-related organization such as Ducks Unlimited is the possibility of writing grant applications. Experienced participants work with the people in charge of a local organization to write grant applications to government or private funding sources. There are many sources of funding for animal-related projects. Each grant application is an excellent opportunity for a young person to be part of the planning process for projects working with animals or animal habitats, and to be hired. Some funding programs have shorter deadlines than a year, so a decision might be made to fund a program beginning in as little as three months.

Filling out grant applications requires concentration and paying attention to details. It's a good skill to learn. So is the skill of writing project proposals. A school guidance counselor may be able to help a student get school credits for business course assignments after completing grant applications. A young person could apply these skills in future projects for the same organization or other groups. These skills will also be useful when applying for college funding for studying biology and agricultural sciences, or arts grants for projects with an animal-related theme.

AGRICULTURAL TECHNOLOGY WORK

The experience of working on a family farm is good training for work as an agricultural technician. It takes one or two years of formal training at an agricultural college or community college to complete a certificate to qualify as an agricultural technician or technologist. These technical workers do the animal handling and feeding for scientist researchers and much of the data entry and computer record keeping as well.

Working outdoors every day, in all kinds of weather, can be a challenge. It's good to meet the needs of animals that rely on human care for daily needs. Working on a family farm can provide young people with a solid foundation for future prospects as agricultural technicians.

There are a variety of jobs in the private sector, but one of the biggest employers is in public service, in the U.S. Department of Agriculture (USDA). The USDA Agricultural Marketing Services (AMS) Web site (http://www.ams.usda.gov) maintains links to student career experience programs as well as employment opportunities in dairy, livestock, and poultry programs. Another USDA branch, the Economic Research Service (ERS), has a Web site (http://www.ers.usda.gov/AboutERS/Employment) with information about their Student Temporary Employment Program. Check out the U.S. Fish and Wildlife Services Web site (http://www.fws.gov/jobs) for their hiring programs. Other countries have similar government programs.

CITIZEN SCIENCE

There are plenty of ways to be involved in citizen science programs with an animal theme. Banding birds and tagging butterflies requires many volunteers for each scientist in a program. Bird counts rely on hundreds of bird-watchers supplementing the observations of each field biologist. Habitat restoration involves hands-on work clearing trash from creeks or

MAKING CONTACTS

Teenagers building a career or business working with animals should keep track of all professional and personal contacts along the way. Every boss or client has something to teach a young worker, and one might even agree to become a mentor. In addition, there is no substitute for a personal introduction from one satisfied pet owner to another new client. An introduction from a veterinarian might assist a young person in getting the perfect job interview. Reference letters can help a student's admission application for college and perhaps even a scholarship award.

pulling invasive vines out of parks. Working in citizen science or at an animal-themed event can be hard work, whether it earns a wage or not. The experience is a good addition to a résumé. It's also a great way to meet working biologists and professors and get reference letters from the scientists in charge. It might even lead to a college or university fellowship for a stipend.

There are benefits to volunteering for a youth conference for biodiversity, environmental justice or empowerment groups, or green groups. The events will be great learning experiences. Furthermore, the next time a group organizes a conference or a program, the few jobs for pay are likely to go to an experienced volunteer. Volunteering for the Nature Conservancy, National Audubon Society, or the Sierra Club for a few weekends in the winter increases a student's chances of being among the people hired for summer projects. Short-term jobs can lead to scholarship programs at universities or careers in environmental activism and sciences.

These teens test river water quality for fish and invertebrates. Taking samples and making records is an important part of environmental work. It's possible to be efficient and effective while still enjoying the company of friends doing outdoor work.

Being part of citizen science and animal activism doesn't take time or energy away from working for money. These programs fit in well with high school and college studies. They complement part-time work. They are a good example of how recreation combines with working and special events. These programs offer the knowledge, business contacts, and opportunities young people need to make their own part-time work or begin a satisfying professional career. Citizen science is only one of many ways that young people who care for animals can have fun while building careers as scientists or entrepreneurs fitting into the local economy.

GLOSSARY

ANIMAL RESCUE Programs that save domestic animals treated badly by people or injured wild animals.

ARTIFICIAL INSEMINATION Conception assisted by doctors instead of letting animals breed.

BONDABLE Having no criminal record and a good credit rating.

BUSKERS Street performers and professional entertainers who often work with animals and music.

CATCH-AND-RELEASE Catching a fish and immediately releasing it as a way to help the fish survive so that fish populations will not become depleted.

CHARISMATIC MEGAFAUNA Large animal species, such as the California condor, bald eagle, and giant panda, that have special appeal to the public and to conservationists and environmentalists.

CITIZEN SCIENCE Programs that use ordinary citizens as volunteers to assist biologists and other scientists in gathering information and statistics.

COMPETITIVE PRICES Prices that are comparable to similar goods or services available.

CRUELTY-FREE Allowing free movement of farm animals in environments with appropriate stimulation, instead of overcrowding or restraining animals in stacked cages.

ENDANGERED SPECIES A type of animal or plant that is in great danger of becoming extinct.

ENTREPRENEUR A person who starts a new business.

ETHICAL BUSINESS A business that operates with consideration for the community and the environment.

FREE RANGE Being allowed to walk around freely in a shelter and a fenced yard, instead of cooped up in small cages.

HABITAT The natural home or environment for an animal or plant.

HATCHERY A place where scientists allow fish eggs to hatch.

INVASIVE SPECIES A species (plant, animal, or other organism) that is not native to a particular ecosystem and whose introduction to that system (usually by humans) can cause economic or environmental harm or harm to human health.

PADDOCK A fenced yard for keeping large farm animals, such as horses and cattle.

PELT The skin of a fur-bearing animal.

SPECIES-AT-RISK An animal or plant species that might not be formally called endangered but is at risk for no longer surviving in a local area.

STABLE LADS Workers who clean stables and groom horses. They can be male or female and young or elderly.

SUSTAINABLE RESOURCE MANAGEMENT
A business plan to maintain the soil, plants, and animals of the local environment instead of using up and destroying resources.

TEMPERAMENTAL
Fussy or short-tempered, often used to describe animals that are sometimes calm and sometimes dangerous, such as a bull or a pit bull dog.

TERRARIUM
A sealed transparent container in which plans or living organisms are grown.

UNIVERSITY EXTENSION
Short-term, affordable courses and programs that are run through a university, intended for the general public instead of regularly enrolled full-time students.

WILD ANIMAL REHABILITATION
Programs that rescue injured wild animals and retrain them if necessary to survive on their own after release.

FOR MORE INFORMATION

Cool Works
P.O. Box 272
513 Highway 89
Gardiner, MT 59030
(406) 848-1195
Web site: http://www.coolworks.com
This employment service focuses on jobs in interesting places
across the United States, with particular emphasis on jobs in
national parks and outdoor jobs as guides, ranch workers,
and in conservation.

FarmStart
P.O. Box 1875
Guelph, ON N1H 6Z9
Canada
(519) 836-7046
Web site: http://www.farmstart.ca
The objective of FarmStart is to support and encourage a new
generation of farmers to develop locally based, ecologi-
cally sound, and economically viable agricultural enterprises. FarmStart encourages new farmers to engage in
entrepreneurial strategies that creatively turn challenges
into opportunities.

GoodWork Canada
People and Planet
P.O. Box 21006 RPO Ottawa South

Ottawa ON K1S 5N1
Canada
(613) 744-3392
Web site: http://www.goodworkcanada.ca
GoodWork Canada maintains listings of jobs, contracts,
     directorships, internships, and volunteering for green
     businesses.

North East Workers on Organic Farms (NEWOOF)

New England Small Farm Institute (NESFI)
275 Jackson Street
Belchertown, MA 01007
(413) 323-4531
Web site: http://www.smallfarm.org/newoof
The New England Small Farm Institute operates NEWOOF
     to encourage more sustainable regional agriculture.
     NESFI is a nonprofit organization that provides infor-
     mation and training for aspiring and beginning farm-
     ers and those transitioning to organic methods.

U.S. Department of Agriculture (USDA)

1400 Independence Avenue SW
Washington, DC 20250
(202) 720-2791
Web site: http://www.usda.gov
USDA service centers across the country are locations
     where citizens can access the services provided by the
     Farm Service Agency, Natural Resources Conservation
     Service, and Rural Development agencies. The USDA
     Web site has a page (http://offices.sc.egov.usda.gov/
     locator/app) that will provide the address of a USDA
     service center and other agency offices serving your

area, along with information on how to contact them by phone and mail.

U.S. Fish & Wildlife Service (FWS)

Division of Information Resources & Technology
     Management
4401 North Fairfax Drive, Suite 340
Arlington, VA 22203
(800) 344-WILD (9453)
Web site: http://www.fws.gov
The FWS is a bureau within the U.S. Department of the Interior. Its primary mission is to conserve, protect, and enhance fish, wildlife, plants, and all habitats for the benefit of all Americans.

U.S. Forest Service

1400 Independence Avenue SW
Washington, DC 20250-0003
(800) 832-1355
Web site: http://www.fs.fed.us/fsjobs
The Forest Service, an agency of the USDA, employs many people in career positions as foresters, technicians, and biological scientists, with many opportunities for student employment and volunteer projects. On their Web site, click on the "Contact Us/FAQ" page and the "For Students and Parents" page for information about youth employment.

Workaway

Web site: http://www.workaway.info
On the Workaway Web site, registered members can join the international lists of volunteer workers traveling to new places and of host families and organizations. Volunteers

do five hours of work per day in exchange for food and accommodation with host families.

World Wide Opportunities on Organic Farms (WWOOF)

654 Fillmore Street
San Francisco, CA 94117
(415) 621-3276
Web site: http://www.wwoofusa.org
WWOOF is an international organization that arranges for volunteers to find placement on organic farms. The volunteers stay for a few weeks or up to several months doing work for a prearranged number of hours per day, in exchange for food and shelter with the host family. Each national organization runs its own programs, and volunteers may travel internationally.

WEB SITES

Due to the changing nature of Internet links, Rosen Publishing has developed an online list of Web sites related to the subject of this book. This site is updated regularly. Please use this link to access the list:

http://www.rosenlinks.com/MMN/Pets

FOR FURTHER READING

Animal Jobs Direct. *Working with Animals.* Raleigh, NC: Lulu Enterprises, 2009.

Aubrey, Sarah B. *Starting and Running Your Own Small Farm Business.* North Adams, MA: Storey Publishing, 2008.

Field, Shelly. *Career Opportunities in Working with Animals.* New York, NY: Ferguson, 2011.

Guillain, Charlotte. *Jobs If You Like Animals.* Portsmouth, NH: Heinemann, 2012.

Hams, Fred. *The Practical Guide to Keeping Chickens, Ducks, Geese & Turkeys: A Directory of Poultry Breeds and How to Keep Them.* Leicester, England: Lorenz Books, 2012.

Hansen, Geoff, and Chuck Wooster. *Living With Sheep: Everything You Need to Know to Raise Your Own Flock.* Guildford, CT: Lyons Press, 2007.

Hollow, Michele C., and William P. Rives. *The Everything Guide to Working with Animals: From Dog Groomer to Wildlife Rescuer—Tons of Great Jobs for Animal Lovers.* Avon, MA: Adams Media, 2009.

Klimesh, Richard, and Cherry Hill. *Horse Hoof Care.* North Adams, MA: Storey Publishing, 2008.

Lee, Mary. *Opportunities in Animal and Pet Care Careers.* Columbus, OH: McGraw-Hill, 2008.

Miller, Louise. *Careers for Nature Lovers & Other Outdoor Types.* New York, NY: McGraw-Hill, 2008.

Pavlides, Merope. *Animal-Assisted Interventions for Individuals with Autism.* London, England: Jessica Kingsley Publishers, 2008.

Sletto, Kathyrn A. *Keeping Watch: 30 Sheep, 24 Rabbits, 2 Llamas, 1 Alpaca, and a Shepherdess with a Day Job.* Wadena, MN: Borealis Books, 2010.

Steingold, Fred. *Legal Forms for Starting and Running a Small Business.* Berkeley, CA: Nolo, 2012.

Thornton, Kim Campbell. *Careers with Dogs: The Comprehensive Guide to Finding Your Dream Job.* Irvine, CA: BowTie Press, 2011.

Ussery, Harvey. *The Small-Scale Poultry Flock.* White River Junction, VT: Chelsea Green Publishing, 2011.

Vaughan, Cathy. *How to Start a Home-Based Pet-Sitting and Dog-Walking Business.* Guilford, CT: Globe Pequot Press, 2011.

Ward, Fay. *The Cowboy at Work: All About His Job and How He Does It.* Whitefish, MT: Literary Licensing, LLC, 2011.

Whitehead, Sarah. *The City Dog: The Essential Guide for City Dwellers and Their Dogs.* Neptune City, NJ: Octopus, 2008.

Wilkie, Rhonda. *Livestock/Deadstock: Working with Farm Animals from Birth to Slaughter.* Philadelphia, PA: Temple University Press, 2010.

Wingfield, Wayne E. *Veterinary Disaster Medicine: Working Animals.* Mississauga, ON, Canada: Wiley-Blackwell, 2009.

BIBLIOGRAPHY

Beach, Gloria. *How to Land a Top-Paying Animal Husbandry Managers Job*. Ruislip, England: Tebbo, 2012.

Blue, Madison. "Every Stitch Counts." *Canadian Wildlife*, May-June 2012, p. 38.

Born Free Foundation. "Get Involved." Retrieved July 20, 2012 (http://www.bornfree.org.uk/get-involved).

Canadian Parks and Wilderness Society. "Get Involved." CPWS: British Columbia Chapter. Retrieved August 5, 2012 (http://cpawsbc.org/campaigns/campaign -school).

Christen, Carol, and Richard B. Bolles. *What Color Is Your Parachute? For Teens*. 2nd ed. Berkeley, CA: Ten Speed Press, 2010.

Cornell University. "Animal Careers." May 8, 2012. Retrieved July 25, 2012 (http://animalcareers.cornell.edu).

DeNapoli, Dyan. *The Great Penguin Rescue*. New York, NY: Free Press/Simon and Schuster, 2010.

Devantier, Alecia T., and Carol A. Turkington. *Extraordinary Jobs with Animals*. New York, NY: Ferguson, 2006.

Elrod, Selena. "Contact Us." K9 Design. Retrieved July 25, 2012 (http://www.k9design.ca).

Ferguson Publishing. *Animal Careers: What Can I Do Now? Exploring Careers for Your Future*. New York, NY: Ferguson, 2010.

Field, Sally. *Career Opportunities in Working with Animals.* New York, NY: Checkmark Books/Infobase Publishing, 2010.

Galat, Joan Marie. "From Reading to Writing Astronomy." Sci-Why, May 10, 2011. Retrieved July 27, 2012 (http://sci-why.blogspot.ca/2011/04/from-reading-to-writing-astronomy.html).

Gilkerson, Linda. *Self-Employment from Dream to Reality: An Interactive Workbook for Starting Your Small Business.* 3rd ed. Saint Paul, MN: JIST Publishing, 2008.

Green, Gail. *Animals and Teens: The Ultimate Guide.* Blue Ridge Summit, PA: Scarecrow Press, 2008.

Greenland, Paul R., and AnnaMarie L. Sheldon. *Career Opportunities in Conservation and the Environment.* New York, NY: Ferguson/Facts On File, 2007.

Greenpeace. "Work for Greenpeace International." Greenpeace International. Retrieved July 10, 2012 (http://www.greenpeace.org/international/en/about/jobs).

Johanson, Paula. "Waiatt Bay, Quadra Island." *Kayak Yak,* August 4, 2011. Retrieved July 20, 2012 (http://kayakyak.blogspot.ca/2011/08/waiatt-bay-quadra-island.html).

Kaplan, Melissa. "Animal Related Careers." Herp Care Collection, February 27, 2012. Retrieved July 18, 2012 (http://www.anapsid.org/resources/jobs.html).

Libal, Joyce. *Rural Teens and Animal Raising: Large and Small Pets.* Broomall, PA: Mason Crest Publishers, 2007.

Marcus, Erik. *Vegan: The New Ethics of Eating.* Ithaca, NY: McBooks Press, 2001.

Moneo, Shannon. "Havanese Day." *Boulevard*, August 2012, p. 36.

Montana Trappers Association. "Fur Farming." Montana Trappers, 2012. Retrieved August 15, 2012 (http://www.montanatrappers.org/management/fur-farming.htm).

Stewart, Liz. *Vault Career Guide to Veterinary and Animal Careers.* New York, NY: Vault, 2008.

Thayer, Helen. "Mission Statement." *Ka Design.* Retrieved August 2, 2012 (http://www.k9design.ca).

United States Attorney's Office, District of Alaska. "Master Guide Sentenced for Big Game Guiding Offense." United States Department of Justice, August 28, 2012. Retrieved August 29, 2012 (http://www.justice.gov/usao/ak/news/2012/August_2012/Joe%20Norbert%20Hendricks.html).

Woodcock, Bruce. "Careers with Animals." Careers and Employability Services, University of Kent. 2012. Retrieved July 20, 2012 (http://www.kent.ac.uk/careers/animalman.htm).

INDEX

ABOUT THE AUTHOR

For more than twenty years, Paula Johanson has worked as a writer, teacher, and editor. Her nonfiction books on science, health, and literature include *Jobs in Sustainable Agriculture* and *Fish: From the Catch to Your Table.* An accredited teacher, she has written curriculum educational materials. A long-time animal owner herself, Johanson learned to give insulin shots to her landlady's diabetic cat and taught the dog to walk on a leash.

PHOTO CREDITS